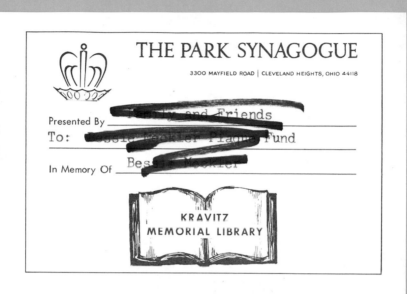
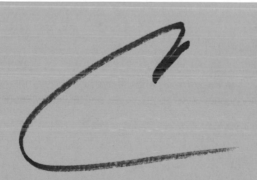

A Festival of Jewish Cooking

בָּרוּךְ אַתָּה יְיָ
אֱלֹהֵינוּ מֶלֶךְ
הָעוֹלָם
הַמּוֹצִיא לֶחֶם
מִן הָאָרֶץ:

Blessed art Thou,
O Lord our God,
King of the universe,
Who brings forth
bread from the
earth.

A Festival of Jewish Cooking

Delicious holiday recipes treasured by generations of Jewish families

collected and designed by
Carole Lowenstein

published by
Herder and Herder

1971
HERDER AND HERDER
232 Madison Avenue, New York 10016

Library of Congress Catalog Card Number: 70-16550c
Copyright 1971 by Herder and Herder, Inc.
Manufactured in the United States

to my
Yiddishe
Momme

With Love

FOREWORD

In this cookbook I have tried to group certain dishes by holiday; they are not absolute, since many recipes are used all year long. I've also selected only the major holidays. The holiest, Yom Kippur, even though a day of fasting, is included because of the foods traditionally prepared before and after its observance. Many recipes have been up-dated to accomodate modern cooks. My thanks to many friends and relatives, and especially to my mother and father. So - read, eat, and enjoy!

table of contents

SABBATH

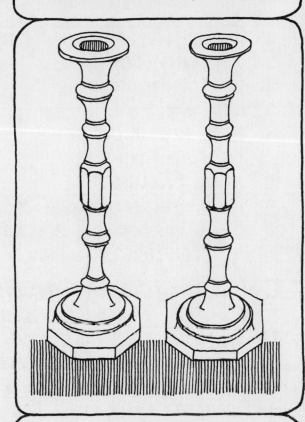

שבת

The Sabbath is the weekly day of rest; all forms of labor are forbidden. There are lights, prayers, and elaborate meals. The Torah is studied at the Synagogue.

gefilte fish

4 lbs. whitefish, pike, carp, or other freshwater fish
4 medium onions
3 tsp. salt
1 tsp. white pepper
1 tsp. sugar
2 eggs, beaten
3 tbsp. matzoh meal or cracker crumbs
6 cups water   2 carrots, sliced
    fish heads, skin, + bones

Grind the fish and an onion using a fine blade. Place in a wooden bowl; stir in eggs, ½ the salt and pepper, sugar, ½ cup water, and matzoh meal. Chop until finely textured. Place fish head, skin, and bones in a large, deep saucepan. Slice in remaining onions; add carrots and rest of water, salt, and pepper. Bring to a boil. Shape the chopped fish with wet hands into 2" balls. Carefully place in the saucepan. Cover and cook over low heat for 1½ hours, shaking saucepan frequently, adding water if needed. Adjust seasoning carefully. Remove fish; strain stock over fish. Chill and serve with horseradish.

CHALLAH

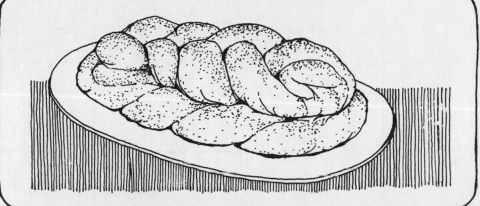

1 cake compressed yeast	3 ¾ cups sifted flour
⅔ cup lukewarm water	1 tsp. salt
2 eggs, slightly beaten	1 egg yolk, slightly beaten
¼ cup sugar	1 tbsp. water
¼ cup vegetable oil	Poppy seeds

Dissolve yeast in lukewarm water. Add eggs, sugar, and oil. Sift flour and salt once, measure; add to yeast mixture; mix well. Turn out on a lightly floured board and knead until smooth (about 5 minutes). Place in a greased bowl. Cover and allow to rise in a warm place until double in bulk. Punch down dough and allow to rise again until light (about 1 hour). Divide the dough into 3 equal parts. Form into balls and cover; allow to stand 15 minutes. Shape each piece into a strip 15" long. Braid the 3 strips together and seal ends. Place on greased baking sheet. Cover and allow to rise until light (about 1½ hours). Brush top with combined egg yolk + water. Sprinkle with poppy seeds. Bake at 350° F. for 45 minutes to 1 hour, until golden.

knaidlach

2 eggs
½ tsp. salt
½ cup matzoh meal
2 tbsp. melted fat
1 tbsp. soup stock
   or water

Separate eggs. Beat yolks, salt, soup stock, and melted fat together. Stir in matzoh meal. Beat egg whites until stiff; fold into yolk mixture. Chill at least 1 hour. Shape into balls and drop into boiling chicken soup. Cover and cook for 30 minutes.

chicken soup

1 5-6 lb. chicken
  feet, neck, and giblets
3 quarts water
1 tbsp. salt
1 large onion, halved
1 parsnip, scraped
2 stalks celery and tops
  few sprigs parsely or
              parsely root
2 carrots, scraped & cut
1 leek
1 sprig of dill

Place the disjointed chicken
and parts into salted water.
Cover and bring to a boil.
Skim the top. Add the
vegetables; cover and simmer
until chicken is tender, about
2-3 hours. Strain the soup.
Chicken may be served
separately.

KASHA VARNISHKES

1 cup medium
   buckwheat groats
1 egg, beaten
1¾ cups boiling
   water
1 tsp. salt

6 tbsp. chicken fat
2 onions, diced
2 cups bowknot
   noodles, cooked
salt and pepper,
   to taste

Cook the groats and egg over low heat until grains are separate. Add water and salt. Cover and cook over low heat about 10 - 15 minutes. Melt fat and sauté onions until golden. Mix noodles, groats, salt, and pepper together lightly, and heat before serving - usually with meat dishes.

GEHAKTE LEBER

½ cup chicken fat   2 eggs, hard-boiled
2 medium onions   2 or 3 soda crackers
1 lb. liver (beef   1 tsp. salt
   or chicken)   pepper to taste

Melt ¼ cup of fat; sauté onions
until golden, set aside. Melt rest
of fat in same pan; sauté liver
about 5-10 minutes. Grind all
together, including eggs and soda
crackers. Adjust seasonings. Chill.

stuffed kishke

BEEF CASING CUT INTO 10"-12" LENGTHS
1 CUP FLOUR
4 TBSP. MATZOH MEAL
1 TSP. SALT
¼ TSP. PEPPER
1½ TSP. PAPRIKA
1 GRATED ONION
½ CUP CHICKEN FAT, MELTED

WASH AND CLEAN THE CASING.
SCRAPE THOROUGHLY, WASH AGAIN
AND DRY. TIE ONE END OF EACH
LENGTH TIGHTLY. MIX STUFFING
INGREDIENTS TOGETHER; STUFF
LIGHTLY, NOT FULL, TO ALLOW
FOR EXPANSION. TIE OTHER END.
DROP INTO BOILING WATER FOR
5 MINUTES; REMOVE CAREFULLY
AND DRAIN. ROAST AT 350°F.
FOR TWO HOURS, BASTING OFTEN.
BETTER, IF ROASTED ALONG WITH
POULTRY OR BEEF.

potato kugel

2 cups grated raw potatoes, drained
1 large onion, grated
1 large carrot
2 eggs, beaten
¼ cup flour
¼ cup matzoh meal
1 tsp. baking powder
1½ tsp. salt
   pepper to taste
4 tbsp. chicken fat

Grate potatoes, onions, and the carrot; add eggs, dry ingredients, and only 2 tbsp. of fat. Mix together well. Pour into greased baking dish. Pour remaining fat on top. Bake at 375°F. about 1-1½ hours, until top is crisp and brown.

ROSH HASHONAH

The Jewish New Year is a time of reflection, prayers, and renewal.

ראש השנה

Shofar

(Ram's Horn — blown at the beginning of Rosh Hashonah and at the end of Yom Kippur.)

יום כפור

The Day of Atonement is the holiest day of the year. Jews fast all day in an act of repentance.

YOM KIPPUR

carrot tzimmes

1 large piece brisket or flanken
1 large bunch carrots, sliced crosswise
½ cup brown sugar
1 tsp. salt
½ tsp. ginger
  dash of pepper
3 large sweet potatoes, diced
THICKENING: 2 tbsp. flour
            2 tbsp. chicken fat
            1 cup meat stock

Brown meat in a dutch oven; pour off excess fat. Add boiling water to cover. Cover and simmer 1 hour. Add carrots, ginger, salt, and pepper. Cover and cook 30 minutes. Add sweet potatoes, brown sugar; cover and cook another hour. Heat flour until pale brown; stir in fat; slowly add stock, stirring constantly. When thick, pour over tzimmes. Bake at 350°F. about 1½ hours, until browned.

KREPLACH

| 2 cups flour | 2 eggs |
| ½ tsp. salt | 2 tbsp. water |

Place flour on board and make a well in the center. Drop eggs, water, and salt into it. Work into the flour and knead the dough until it is smooth and elastic. Flour the board lightly and roll dough as thin as possible. Cut into 3" squares. Put a tablespoon of filling in the center of each square. Fold one corner over to form a triangle. Using some water as a seal, press edges together lightly. Cook kreplach in rapidly boiling salted water or soup for 20 minutes. Drain well. If served as a side dish, may also be browned in oven or fried.

CHOICE OF FILLINGS: ABOUT 2 CUPS WORTH

MEAT: cooked or fresh ground meat sautéed with onions; seasoned.

POTATO: mashed potatoes with sautéed onions and seasoned.

CHEESE: cottage or pot cheese mixed with egg and seasonings.

KASHA: kasha cooked and mixed with sautéed onion and seasoned.

13

sponge cake

6 eggs, separated
1½ cups fine sugar
2 tbsp. water
2 tsp. lemon juice
1 tsp. grated
   orange rind
1 tsp. grated
   lemon rind

1 tsp. vanilla or
   almond extract
¼ tsp. salt
½ tsp. cream
   of tartar
1½ cups sifted
   flour

Beat the yolks, gradually adding the sugar, beating until very thick and light. Add water, juice, rinds, and flavoring. Beat well and set aside. Beat whites until frothy, adding the salt and cream of tartar. Beat stiff enough to hold peaks. Very gently fold beaten whites and sifted flour alternately into yolk mixture. Place in an ungreased tube pan. Bake about one hour at 325°F. Invert pan and cool.

LEKACH

4 EGGS

1 CUP SUGAR

1 CUP HONEY

½ CUP STRONG BLACK COFFEE

2 TBSP. SALAD OIL

3½ CUPS FLOUR

2 TSP. BAKING POWDER

1 TSP. BAKING SODA

¼ TSP. NUTMEG

¼ TSP. GROUND CLOVES

½ tsp. GROUND ALLSPICE

½ TSP. GINGER

1 TSP. CINNAMON

PINCH SALT

½ CUP CHOPPED NUTS

½ CUP RAISINS OR CURRANTS

½ CUP CITRON OR CANDIED FRUITS

3 TBSP. BRANDY (APRICOT)

¼ CUP ORANGE MARMALADE

HALVED ALMONDS FOR TOP

BEAT EGGS. ADD SUGAR GRADUALLY, BEATING UNTIL CREAMY AND LIGHT. COMBINE HONEY AND COFFEE. STIR IN OIL. COMBINE WITH THE EGG MIXTURE AND BEAT WELL. SIFT TOGETHER FLOUR, BAKING POWDER, BAKING SODA, AND SPICES. ADD GRADUALLY TO EGG MIXTURE, BLENDING THOROUGHLY. STIR NUTS, RAISINS, BRANDY, CANDIED FRUITS, AND MARMALADE THROUGH THE BATTER. LINE TWO GREASED LOAF PANS (10 ¼" X 3 ⅝" X 2 ⅝") WITH WAXED PAPER. HALF FILL EACH PAN WITH BATTER; SPRINKLE WITH ALMONDS. BAKE AT 300°F. FOR 1 ¼ HOURS.

TEIGLACH

1½ - 2 cups flour
½ tsp. salt
½ tsp. baking powder
2 eggs, lightly beaten
2 tbsp. oil
1 cup honey

½ cup brown sugar
1 tsp. ground ginger
1 cup nutmeats
½ cup chopped
candied fruit
(optional)

Make a dough by mixing the eggs with the oil, adding flour, salt, and baking powder. Add enough flour to make a dough that can be handled. Knead smooth. Roll and twist into strips until about ½" thick. Cut into ½" lengths. Place on a well-greased shallow pan and bake at 375° about 10 minutes, until golden, shaking pan occasionally to separate balls. Meanwhile, bring honey, sugar, and ginger to a boil, cooking over low heat for 5 minutes. Add baked pastry, nuts, and fruits. Cook and stir over low heat using a wooden spoon until thick and browned, about 5 minutes. Turn out on a wet wooden board. Cool slightly. Dip hands in ice water and form into 2" balls.

MANDELBROT

4 cups flour
2 tsp. baking powder
pinch of salt
1 cup sugar
4 eggs
½ cup salad oil

2 tsp. vanilla flavor
1 tsp. almond flavor
1 cup cut almonds
1 cup cherries or candied fruit
1 grated lemon rind
1 grated orange rind

Sift flour, baking powder, and salt into a bowl. Put sugar in another bowl and beat in eggs, one at a time. Add oil, lemon, and orange rinds, vanilla and almond flavorings. Alternately add flour, almonds, and fruit, to the egg mixture, mixing thoroughly. Knead well on a lightly floured board. Divide dough into eight rolls about 1" high, 3" long, and 2" wide. Brush with milk or cream to glaze. Bake on a greased cookie sheet in a 350°F. oven for 20-30 minutes. Remove from oven. Slice each roll at ½" intervals in a diagonal pattern. Place slices, cut side down, on two cookie sheets. Return to the oven and bake at 275°F. for 20 minutes on each side, or until lightly browned and crisp.

SUKKOT

סכות

The Feast of Tabernacles celebrates the ancient fruit harvest in the Holy Land. Sukkot, or temporary booths, are hung with fruits and flowers.

KICHLECH

2 EGGS

1 TBSP. OIL

2 TSP. VANILLA

1 TBSP. SUGAR

2 TSP. LEMON JUICE

½ TSP. SALT

1½ - 2 CUPS FLOUR

½ TSP. BAKING POWDER

POWDERED SUGAR

BEAT EGGS WELL. SLOWLY ADD OIL, LEMON JUICE, VANILLA, SUGAR, AND SALT. SIFT FLOUR AND BAKING POWDER. ADD FLOUR; MIX THOROUGHLY; KNEAD LIGHTLY. ROLL OUT ON A LIGHTLY FLOURED BOARD AND CUT INTO DIAMOND SHAPES. FRY IN DEEP FAT UNTIL GOLDEN. DRAIN; SPRINKLE WITH THE POWDERED SUGAR.

chopped herring

DRAIN:
  1 8-oz. jar herring
      fillets in wine
      sauce
SOAK IN DRAINED
SAUCE:
  1 slice rye bread
  1 slice pumpernickel
GRIND TOGETHER:
  drained herring
  1 large onion
  2 large stalks of
    celery
  1 small green
    pepper
  1 medium carrot
  2 peeled apples
  2 hard-boiled eggs
  the soaked bread,
    unsqueezed
ADD:
  sugar to taste
  dash of pepper
IF TOO MOIST:
  add a few ground
    up crackers

holipshkes

18 cabbage leaves
1½ lbs. chopped beef
½ cup water
1 egg
½ cup instant rice
½ tsp. onion salt
1 can tomato sauce
1 can water

1 diced onion
½ cup brown sugar
2 tbsp. honey
6 crushed ginger-
 snap cookies
juice from ½ lemon
½ diced apple
handful of raisins

Steam cabbage leaves until slightly wilted. Mix chopped beef with rice, salt, ½ cup water, and egg. Roll a heaping tablespoon of meat mixture in each cabbage leaf. Place rolls in a pan in a sauce made of tomato sauce, water, brown sugar, honey, ginger-snaps, diced onion, lemon juice, the diced apple, raisins. Cook about 3 hours in a dutch oven on top of the stove, basting occasionally.

STRUDEL

½ lb. sweet butter   FILLING:
½ pt. sour cream   cinnamon & sugar
2 cups flour   white raisins
                      apricot or peach
                         preserves
                      cocoanut
                      chopped nuts

Blend butter, flour, and sour cream. Wrap in wax paper and refrigerate overnight. Remove dough and cut into 4 pieces, keeping unused portions refrigerated until use. Roll into a rectangle on floured cloth. Sprinkle along edge closest to you with cinnamon and sugar, cocoanut, raisins, chopped nuts, and preserves. Roll carefully, like a jelly roll; seal ends. Bake on a greased cookie sheet about ½ hr., at 350°F. until golden. Cool; cut on an angle with sharp knife.

CHANUKAH

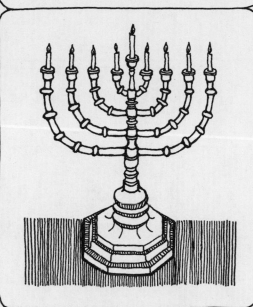

חנוכה

Chanukah commemorates the victory of the Maccabees over the Syrians, and the rededication of the Temple, where oil which was to burn only one day then miraculously burned for eight. Thus, one candle is added to the menorah nightly.

matzoh latkes

¾ cup matzoh meal   dash cinnamon
½ tsp. salt   3 eggs, separated
1 tbsp. sugar   1 cup milk, warm

Stir warm milk into matzoh meal. Add, salt, sugar, cinnamon, and the beaten egg yolks. Add stiffly beaten egg whites and fry by tablespoons in hot butter. Serve hot with preserves, sour cream, or sprinkled with sugar and cinnamon.

potato latkes

3 cups grated raw
   potatoes, drained
1 onion, grated
1 tsp. salt
2 eggs, beaten

3 tbsp. matzoh
   meal or flour
½ tsp. baking
    powder
oil for frying

Mix all ingredients together until smooth. Drop by tablespoons into hot oil in a skillet. Fry on both sides until brown. Drain well. Serve hot with applesauce or sour cream.

FRUIT COMPOTE

1   11-oz. package mixed dried
     fruit
⅔ cup brown sugar
½ cup raisins (light & dark)
½ orange or lemon, sliced
     paper thin, then halved
2 tbsp. lemon juice
1 tsp. whole cloves
1 inch stick cinnamon

Combine ingredients in a 1½
quart casserole. Add water
to cover, about 2½ cups.
Cover and bake at 350°F. for
about 1½ hours. Cool.

MUSHROOM & BARLEY SOUP

10 fresh mushrooms, or dried mushrooms, soaked
4 tbsp. large pearl barley   2 tsp. salt
½ cup dried lima beans   ¼ tsp. pepper
¼ cup diced celery   2 quarts water
2 sprigs parsely, chopped   ½ cup milk
¼ cup diced carrots   2 tbsp. flour
1 medium onion, diced   chopped dill
3 tbsp. butter

Wash mushrooms, barley, and lima beans. Slice mushrooms finely. Add to boiling water the mushrooms, barley, beans, salt, 1½ tbsp. butter, diced celery, parsely, and carrots. Cook for one hour. When soup is simmering, stir slowly every 20 minutes until barley is tender. In a saucepan, melt butter over low heat, and sauté onions. Add flour, stir. Add milk, making a smooth white sauce. When soup is cooked, add white sauce and mix well. Adjust seasoning to taste. Serve hot, garnished with chopped dill.

PURIM

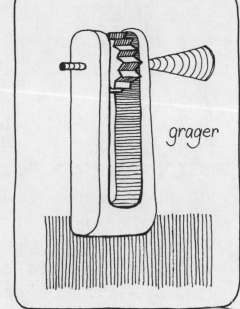

grager

פורים

On this gay holi-
day, the Book of
Esther is read, and
children twirl
their gragers, or
noisemakers, each
time the enemy,
Haman, is said,
to drown out his
name.

piroshki

½ cup butter
½ pint sour cream
1 egg, whole

flour and salt
1 tsp. baking powder
1 egg, beaten

Combine butter, sour cream, whole egg. Sift in the flour, baking powder, and salt. Use enough flour to thicken the mixture so that it can be rolled out very thin. Cut out rings about 2½" in diameter; put one teaspoon of the filling on each; fold over and pinch edges together. Paint with a beaten egg and bake in a fairly hot oven, 425°F., on a well-greased pan until golden.

FILLING:

¼ cup shortening
1 onion, chopped
½ lb. mushrooms, chopped

¼ lb. chicken livers, chopped
2 tsp. salt
dash paprika
freshly ground black pepper

Using half the shortening in a skillet, sauté onions and mushrooms until golden. Set aside. Sauté livers in remaining shortening; combine mixtures and seasonings. Mash smooth. Let cool a while before using.

POTATO KNISHES

¼ CUP CHICKEN FAT
2 MEDIUM ONIONS,
    CHOPPED
PAPRIKA
4 CUPS MASHED
    POTATOES
3 EGGS, BEATEN
¾-1 CUP FLOUR

½ TSP. BAKING POWDER
1 TSP. SALT
DASH PEPPER
2 TBSP. GRATED ONION
2 TBSP. MELTED
    CHICKEN FAT
1 EGG YOLK, DILUTED
    WITH 1 TBSP. WATER

SAUTÉ ONIONS IN CHICKEN FAT, SPRINKLING
WITH PAPRIKA; COOL. MIX TOGETHER
POTATOES, BEATEN EGGS, FLOUR, BAKING
POWDER, SALT, PEPPER, GRATED ONION, AND
MELTED FAT. KNEAD SMOOTH. SHAPE INTO
2" BALLS; PRESS A THUMBHOLE IN THE
CENTER OF EACH BALL AND FILL WITH A
TEASPOON OF THE SAUTÉED ONIONS. CLOSE
OVER FILLING. FLATTEN BALLS SLIGHTLY.
PLACE ON A GREASED SHEET AND BRUSH
WITH EGG YOLK DILUTED WITH WATER.
BAKE AT 350° F. ABOUT 25 MINUTES OR
UNTIL BROWNED.

hamentaschen

1 package yeast
¼ cup scalded milk, cooled
4 tbsp. sugar
1 cup scalded milk, cooled
¼ cup sugar
½ cup melted shortening
½ tsp. salt
2 eggs, beaten
3¾ - 4 cups flour
grated rind of ½ lemon
1 tsp. vanilla

Combine yeast, milk, and the sugar in a cup. Allow to soften for 5 minutes. Combine milk, sugar, shortening, salt, eggs, lemon rind, vanilla, and yeast mixture in a bowl. Add flour gradually, mixing together lightly until a dough is formed. Knead until very smooth. Place in a greased bowl. Cover with a cloth and set aside in a warm place for 2 hours, or until double in bulk. (May be punched down, turned in a bowl, covered,

and refrigerated overnight.)
Now for filling:

2 cups ground poppy seeds
¾ cup milk
½ cup honey
¼ cup brown sugar
⅛ tsp. salt
1 egg, beaten
warm honey for glazing
¼ cup chopped raisins
½ cup chopped almonds

Combine poppy seeds, milk, honey, brown sugar, and salt in a saucepan. Cook over low heat for 5 minutes, stirring constantly. Cool for 15 minutes. Add egg, almond, raisins, and mix well. (Can be sweetened more with ¼ cup currant or raspberry jelly or jam.) Punch down dough and knead for 1 minute. Roll out to 3"-4" circles, ⅛" thick, on lightly floured board. Brush with oil and spread with filling. Fold over edges to form 3-cornered cake. Brush warm honey on top; let rise. Bake at 350°F. for 20-30 minutes.

PASSOVER

פֶּסַח

The eight day festival of Passover recalls the Jews' Exodus from Egypt and their deliverance from slavery. At the traditional Seder meal, the story of freedom, or the Haggadah, is read, and Matzoh and other symbolic foods are eaten.

CHAROSIS

1 tsp. honey
½ cup ground walnuts
1 apple, peeled and grated
3 tbsp. sweet wine
¼ tsp. cinnamon

Mix all together until smooth. Eat with matzohs.

MATZOH BRIE

4 matzohs
4 eggs
1½ tsp. salt
3 tbsp. hot fat

Soak the matzohs in water until soft. Drain and squeeze dry. Beat eggs with the salt. Pour over the matzohs; mix well. Heat fat; pour the mixture into pan. Fry until golden on both sides.

MATZOH KUGEL

3 MATZOHS
4 EGGS, SEPARATED
½ TSP. SALT
¼ CUP MELTED BUTTER
4 APPLES, PEELED + SHREDDED
¼ CUP SUGAR
¼ TSP. CINNAMON
GRATED RIND OF 1 ORANGE
½ CUP RAISINS
½ CUP CHOPPED ALMONDS

BEAT EGG WHITES AND SET ASIDE. SOAK MATZOHS IN WATER; SQUEEZE DRY. ADD REST OF THE INGRE- DIENTS AND MIX THO- ROUGHLY. FOLD IN BEAT- EN EGG WHITES. BAKE IN A WELL-GREASED CASSEROLE AT 350°F. FOR ABOUT 45 MINUTES TO AN HOUR.

COCOANUT MACAROONS

3 egg whites
1 cup sugar
¼ tsp. salt
1 tbsp. lemon juice
1 7-oz. pkg. shredded
             cocoanut

Beat the egg whites, slowly adding the salt and sugar, until the sugar is dissolved and the egg whites are stiff, but not dry. Sprinkle the cocoanut, a small amount at a time, over the whites, folding in gently, and alternating with the lemon juice. Repeat until all of the cocoanut is used. Drop by teaspoons on a cookie sheet lined with plain brown paper. Bake at 350°F. for 12-15 minutes, until golden. Remove and cool on a wire rack.

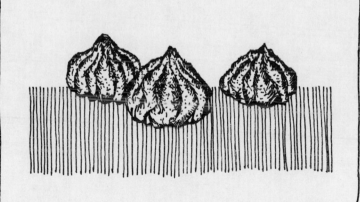

SHAVUOTH

לא תרצח	אנכיהוה אלהיך
לא תנאף	לא יהיה לך
לא תגנב	לא תשא
לא תענה	זכור את יום השבת
לא תחמד	כבד את אביך

שבועות

Shavuoth celebrates
Moses receiving the
Torah and the Ten
Commandments
from the Lord on
Mount Sinai.

lokshen kugel

8 oz. broad noodles, cooked in boiling, salted water,
    and drained
3 eggs, beaten
¼ cup sugar
1 tsp. cinnamon
¼ cup melted butter
¼ tsp. salt
1 tsp. vanilla

½ pint sour cream
½ cup milk
1 lb. creamed cottage
    cheese
1 8-oz. can crushed
    pineapple
handful of raisins

Stir all ingredients together. Pour into a well-buttered baking dish. Bake at 350°F. for an hour, or until top is golden.

fruit borscht

3 cups fresh or dried fruit (any combination may be
    used: cherries, peaches, pears, apricots, etc.)
water to cover (about 1½ quarts)
2 tsp. lemon juice
½ tsp. salt
¼ cup sugar (about)

stick cinnamon
2 tbsp. cornstarch
2 tbsp. cold water
sour cream

Pit the fruit; combine the fruit, water, lemon juice, salt, sugar, and stick cinnamon. Bring to a boil. Cover and simmer for 20 minutes or until fruit is soft. Remove from heat. Remove cinnamon. Put through a sieve or purée in a blender. Return soup to heat and bring to a boil. Make a paste of cornstarch + water. Slowly add to soup, stirring constantly. Cook for 5 mins. Sweeten more if needed. Serve ice-cold with sour cream.

cheese blintzes

1 TEASPOON SUGAR
2 EGGS
2 TBSP. SALAD OIL
1 TSP. VANILLA

1 CUP MILK
¾ CUP SIFTED FLOUR
½ TSP. SALT

BEAT THE EGGS, OIL, SUGAR, VANILLA, AND MILK TOGETHER. ADD FLOUR AND SALT. BEAT SMOOTH. CHILL FOR AT LEAST ONE HOUR. BRUSH HEATED 6"-7" SKILLET WITH MELTED BUTTER. POUR ABOUT 2 TBSP. BATTER INTO PAN, TILT PAN TO SPREAD BATTER TO COVER BOTTOM. COOK ABOUT 1 MINUTE UNTIL LIGHTLY BROWNED ON ONE SIDE ONLY, TURN OUT, BROWN SIDE UP. REPEAT UNTIL BATTER IS USED UP, RE-GREASING PAN AS REQUIRED. PLACE SPOONFUL OF FILLING ON BLINTZE. FOLD IN SIDES; ROLL UP CAREFULLY. TO SERVE: BROWN IN BUTTER ON BOTH SIDES. SERVE HOT WITH SOUR CREAM OR SPRINKLED WITH CINNAMON AND SUGAR.   _filling:_

½ LB. COTTAGE CHEESE
¼ LB. CREAM CHEESE
1 EGG
2 TBSP. SUGAR

½ TSP. SALT
1 TSP. VANILLA EXTRACT
½ TSP. CINNAMON
½ TSP. GRATED LEMON RIND

MATZOH MEAL TO THICKEN

STIR ALL TOGETHER UNTIL SMOOTH, ADDING ENOUGH MATZOH MEAL TO HOLD THE MIXTURE TOGETHER. USE TO FILL THE BLINTZES.

cheesecake

PASTRY:
1 cup sifted flour
¼ cup sugar
dash cinnamon
1 tsp. grated lemon rind
1 tsp. vanilla
1 egg yolk
½ cup butter

CHEESE FILLING:
2½ lb. cream cheese
1¾ cups sugar
3 tbsp. flour
1½ tsp. grated orange rind
1½ tsp. grated lemon rind
½ tsp. vanilla
1 tbsp. lemon juice
5 eggs
2 egg yolks
¼ cup heavy cream

Mix flour, sugar, lemon rind, cinnamon, and vanilla in a bowl. Make a well in the center, add unbeaten egg yolk and butter and work mixture together with your hands until it forms a ball. Wrap in waxed paper and chill in refrigerator for at least one hour. When thoroughly chilled, get a 9" spring-form pan and oil the bottom. Start the oven at 400°F., or moderately hot. Cut off about ¼ of the dough, roll dough directly on bottom of pan ⅛" thick with a rolling pin. Trim the edges evenly. Bake this bottom crust 10 minutes, or until golden. Cool. Divide remaining dough in three sections and roll each part ⅛" thick in a narrow strip on a lightly floured board.

Fit these thin strips around the buttered sides of the spring-form pan and press the joining edges together to line sides completely. Trim top edge of dough neatly so that the dough reaches 3/4 of the height of the pan. NOTE: this amount of dough is exactly right only if it is rolled thin enough. Chill dough in refrigerator until filling is made. Turn your oven up to 550°F., or very hot. Mix cream cheese, sugar, flour, grated orange and lemon rind, vanilla, and lemon juice in a large bowl. Beat until mixture is smooth and well-blended. Drop in the eggs and extra egg yolks one at a time and stir lightly after each addition. Mix in the cream last of all. Pour cheese filling into the pan and bake 10 minutes at this very high temperature. Then reduce heat to 200°F., or very, very low, and continue baking one hour longer. Cool on a cake rack until completely cold. Release the sides of the pan, remove, and serve cold without removing the bottom of the pan.

MISCELLANEOUS RECIPES

kochletin

1 medium onion, grated
1 clove garlic, crushed, or
   garlic powder
2 eggs, beaten
2 tbsp. chopped parsely

¼ cup water
1 tsp. salt
dash pepper
¼ cup matzoh meal (about)
1 lb. ground beef

Mix all together, using enough matzoh meal to hold together. Shape into patties. Fry on both sides in hot fat.

ruglach

4 oz. butter
4 oz. cream cheese } at room temp.
¼ tsp. salt

1 cup flour
1 egg yolk
2 tsp. cream or milk

Beat butter, cheese, and salt together in mixer until smooth
and blended. Work in flour with fingertips or fork to a
smooth dough. Chill overnight. Divide dough into quarters.
Keep unrolled portion in refrigerator until ready to use.
Roll into a circle ⅛" thick on a well-floured board. Cut
into wedges. Place filling at wide end of wedge and roll
to center; curve into crescents. Brush tops only with
egg yolk beaten with cream. Bake at 350° F. about 20
minutes, or until delicately browned.

FILLING:

    1 egg white, stiffly beaten
    ¾ cup ground walnuts
    ¼ cup sugar
    1 tbsp. cinnamon
    1 tsp. vanilla

Mix all together, and use to fill the ruglach.

BAGELS

1 cake of yeast
1½ tsp. sugar
1 cup lukewarm potato water (water in which you've cooked peeled po" tatoes).

2 tbsp. melted shortening
1 tsp. salt
3½ – 4 cups flour
2 eggs

Dissolve yeast and sugar in ⅓ cup of potato water. Sift dry ingredients together. Add yeast mix to the flour; stir. Add melted shortening to remaining water, and add to the flour mix. Drop in eggs and stir briskly to form a dough. Knead until smooth and elastic, about 10 minutes. Add enough flour to make a firm dough. Place dough in a bowl; cover and let rise. Knead again; pinch off pieces and roll between lightly floured hands into ropes the width of a finger and twice the length. Shape into rings, pinching the ends well together. Let stand on a floured board only until they begin to rise. Bring a large pot of sugared water to just below the boiling point. Drop each bagel in one at a time. Cook on one side; turn carefully and cook on the other. Remove gently to a greased baking sheet. Bake at 400°F. about 15 minutes until golden and crusted. If desired, sprinkle with either coarse salt, poppy seeds, sesame seeds, or caraway seeds before baking.

INDEX

kreplach	13
kugel, lokshen	44
kugel, matzoh	39
kugel, potato	9

latkes, matzoh	26
latkes, potato	27
lekach	15

macaroons, cocoanut	40
mandelbrot	17
matzoh brie	38

piroshki	32

ruglach	50

soup, chicken	5
soup, mushroom and barley	29
strudel	23

teiglach	16
tzimmes, carrot	12